# The Baptism with The Holy Spirit

By

## R. A. Torrey

Loki's Publishing

Seattle, WA

# The Baptism with The Holy Spirit

R. A. Torrey

"Wait for the promise of the Father." —Acts 1:4.

"Ye shall be baptized with the Holy Spirit not many days hence." —Acts 1:5.

"Ye shall receive Power after that the Holy Ghost is come upon you."— Acts 1 : 8.

"For to you is the promise, and to your children, and to all that are afar off, even as many as the Lord our God shall call unto Him." —Acts 2:39 R. V.

# The Baptism with The Holy Spirit

R. A. Torrey

# Contents

# The Baptism with The Holy Spirit

# INTRODUCTION

It was a great turning point in my ministry, when, after much thought and study and meditation, I became satisfied that the Baptism with the Holy Spirit was an experience for today and for me, and set myself about obtaining it. Such blessing came to me personally, that I began giving Bible readings on the subject, and with increasing frequency as the years have passed. God in His wondrous grace has so greatly blessed these readings, and so many have asked for them in printed form, convenient for circulation among their friends, that I have decided to write them out in full for publication. It is an occasion of great joy that so many and such excellent books on the person and work of the Holy Spirit have appeared of late. I wish to call especial attention to two of these: "Through the Eternal Spirit," by James Elder Gumming and "The Spirit of Christ," by Andrew Murray.

In the following pages I speak uniformly of the Holy Spirit, but in the quotations from the Bible retain the less desirable phraseology there used — "The Holy Ghost" — except in those instances where the translators themselves varied their usage. Probably most of the readers of this book already know that "the Holy Spirit" and "the Holy Ghost" are

**The Baptism with The Holy Spirit**

simply two different translations of precisely the same Greek words. It seems very unfortunate, and almost unaccountable, that the English revisers did not follow the suggestion of the American Committee, and, for "Holy Ghost", adopt uniformly the rendering "Holy Spirit."

R. A. Torrey

# CHAPTER I

## THE BAPTISM WITH THE HOLY SPIBIT: WHAT IT IS AND WHAT IT DOES

While a great deal is said in these days concerning the Baptism with the Holy Spirit, it is to be feared that there are many who talk about it and pray for it, who have no clear and definite idea of what it is. But the Bible, if carefully studied, will give us a view of this wondrous blessing that is perfectly clear and remarkably definite.

1. We find first of all, that *there are a number of designations in the Bible for this one* experience. In Acts 1:5, Jesus said, "*Ye shall be baptized with the Holy ghost not many days hence.*" In Acts 2:4, when this promise was fulfilled, we read, "*they were all filled with the Holy Ghost.*" In Acts 1:4, the same experience is spoken of as "*the promise of the Father*" and in Luke 24:49 as "*the promise of my Father,*" and "*endued power from on high,*" By a comparison of Acts 10:44, 45, 47 with Acts 11:15, 16, we find that the expressions "*the Holy Spirit fell on them*" and "*the gift of the Holy Ghost,*" and

The Baptism with The Holy Spirit
*"received the Holy Ghost"* are all equivalent to
*"baptized with the Holy Ghost."*

2. We find in the next place, that *the Baptism
with the Holy Spirit is a definite experience of which
one may know whether he has received it or not.* This
is evident from our Savior's command to the
Apostles: "Tarry ye in the city, until ye be endued
with power from on high." (Luke 24:49.) Unless this
enduement with power, or Baptism with the Holy
Ghost, is an experience so definite that one can know
whether he has received it or not, how could they tell
when those commanded days of tarrying were at an
end? The same thing is clear from Paul's very
definite question to the disciples at Ephesus. "Did ye
receive the Holy Ghost when ye believed?" (Acts
19:2, R. V.) Paul evidently expected a definite "yes,"
or a definite "no" for an answer. Unless the
experience is definite, and of such a character that
one can know whether he has received it or not, how
could these disciples answer Paul's question? In point
of fact, they knew they had not "received," or been
"baptized with," the Holy Ghost, and a short time
afterward they knew they had "received," or been
"baptized with," the Holy Ghost. (Acts 19:6.) Ask
many a man today, who prays that he may be
baptized with the Holy Ghost: "Well, my brother, did
you get what you asked? Were you baptized with the
Holy Ghost?" and he would be dumb-founded. He
did not expect anything so definite that he could
answer positively to a question like that, "yes" or

"no." But we find in the Bible none of that vagueness and indefiniteness regarding this subject which we find in much of our modem prayer and speech. The Bible is a very definite book. It is very definite about salvation: so definite that a man who knows his Bible can say positively "yes" or "no" to the question "are you saved." It is equally definite about "the Baptism with the Holy Ghost:" so definite that a man who knows his Bible can say positively, "yes," or "no," to the question, "have you been baptized with the Holy Ghost." There may be those who are saved who do not know it, because they do not understand their Bibles, but it is their privilege to know it. So there may be those who have been Baptized with the Holy Ghost, who do not know the Bible name for what has come to them, but it is their privilege to know.

3. *The Baptism with the Holy Spirit is a work of the Holy Spirit separate and distinct from His regenerating work.* To be regenerated by the Holy Spirit is one thing, to be baptized with the Holy Spirit is something different, something additional. This is evident from Acts 1:5. There Jesus said: "Ye shall be baptized with the Holy Ghost *not many day hence.*" They where not then as yet *"baptized with the Holy Ghost."* But they were *already* regenerated. Jesus Himself had already pronounced them so. In John 15:3, He had said to the same men, "Now are ye clean through the Word." (Comp. Jas. 1:18; 1 Pet. 1:23) and in John 13:10: "Ye are clean, but not all," excepting, by the "but not all," the one unregenerate

man in the Apostolic company, Judas Iscariot, from the statement "Ye are clean." ( See John 13:11.) The Apostles, excepting Judas Iscariot, were then already regenerate men, but they were not yet "baptized with the Holy Ghost." From this it is evident that regeneration is one thing, and that the baptism with the Holy Spirit is something different, something additional. One may be regenerated and still not yet be baptized with the Holy Ghost. The same thing is evident from Acts 8:12-16. Here we find a company of believers who had been baptized. Surely in this company of baptized believers there were some regenerate men. But the record informs us that when Peter and John came down they "prayed for them that they might receive the Holy Ghost: (for *as yet He was fallen upon none of them*)." It is clear then that one may be a believer, may be a regenerate man, and yet not have the Baptism with the Holy Spirit. In other words, the Baptism with the Holy Spirit is something distinct from and beyond His regenerating work. Not every regenerate man has the Baptism with the Holy Spirit, though as we shall see later, every regenerate man may have this Baptism. If a man has experienced the regenerating work of the Holy Spirit he is a saved man, but he is not fitted for service until in addition to this he has received the Baptism with the Holy Spirit.

But while the baptism with the Spirit is an operation of the Holy Spirit separate and distinct from His regenerating work it may and often does occur simultaneously with it. A man may be baptized with the Spirit the moment he is regenerated. It was so in the case of the household of Cornelius. It is so in the case of many today. It would be so in every case in a perfectly normal condition of the Church. The apostles expected that when men were converted and regenerated they should also be baptized with the Holy Spirit at once and fitted for immediate service. (Eph. 1:13; R. V. Acts 3:38, 1 Cor. 12:13; Acts 8:15, 16; 9:17; 19:2: R. V.) In some cases, as at Ephesus, (Acts 19: 1-6) and Samaria, (Acts 8:12-16), because of inadequate instruction, or other reasons, this was not the case. The Ephesus or Samaria condition of affairs seems to be the prevailing condition today and we need to go about asking as Paul did at Ephesus "Have ye received the Holy Ghost since ye believed" (Acts 19:2.), and insisting that regeneration is not enough but, that believers must also be baptized with the Holy Spirit.

4. *The baptism with the Holy Spirit is always connected with testimony and service.* Look carefully at every passage in which the Baptism with the Holy Spirit is mentioned, and you will see that it is connected with, and is for the purpose of, testimony and service. (For example, Acts 1:5,8; 2:4; 4:31, 33.) This will come out very clearly when we come to consider what the Baptism with the Holy Spirit does. The Baptism with the Holy Spirit, is not an experience that God grants to us merely to make us happy. It will indeed bring into our lives a joy such as

we never knew before. But that is not its main purpose. The Baptism with the Spirit is not intended to make us happy but make us effective. We should not look and long for ecstatic experiences, but for power and efficiency for God. The Baptism with the Holy Spirit is not even primarily for the purpose of cleansing from sin, but for the purpose of empowering for service. There is a line of teaching, put forward by a very earnest but mistaken body of people, that has brought the whole doctrine of the Baptism with the Holy Spirit into disrepute. It runs this way: First proposition: there is a further experience (or second blessing) after regeneration, namely, the Baptism with the Holy Spirit. This proposition is true and can be easily proven from the Bible. Second proposition: this Baptism with the Holy Spirit can be instantaneously received. This proposition is also true and can be easily proven from the Bible. Third proposition: this Baptism with the Holy Spirit is the eradication of the sinful nature. This proposition is untrue. Not a line of Scripture can be adduced to show that the Baptism with the Holy Spirit is the eradication of the sinful nature. The conclusion, viz., "the sinful nature can be instantaneously eradicated," drawn from these three propositions, two true and one false, is necessarily false. The purpose of cleansing from sin, but for the Baptism with the Holy Spirit is not primarily for purpose of empowering for service. It is indeed the work of the Holy Spirit to cleanse from sin. Further than this there is a work of the Holy Spirit where the

believer is strengthened with might in the inner man:
that Christ may dwell in his heart by faith . . . that he
might be filled unto all the fullness of God. (Eph. 3:
16-19 R. V.) There is a work of the Holy Spirit of
such a character that the believer is "made free from
the law of sin and death," (Rom. 8:2) and through the
Spirit does "mortify (put to death) the deeds of the
body." (Rom. 8:13.) It is our privilege to so walk,
daily and hourly, in the power of the Spirit, that the
carnal nature is kept in the place of death. But this is
not the Baptism with the Spirit, neither is it the
*eradication* of the sinful nature. It is not something
done once for all, it is something that must be
momentarily maintained. "Walk in the Spirit, and ye
shall not fulfill the lust of the flesh." (Gal 5:16.)

While insisting that the Baptism with the Spirit is
primarily, for the purpose of empowering for service,
it should be added that the Baptism is accompanied
by a great moral uplift. It ought to mean and usually
does means a transformed life as well as a
transformed ministry. (See Acts 2:44-46; 4:31-35.)
This is necessarily so, from the steps one must take to
obtain this blessing. Further than this we cannot
forget that one of the promises on this subject reads:
"He shall baptize you with the Holy Ghost, *and with
fire*," (Matt. 3:11.) When we notice that here fire
seems to be contrasted with water in the earlier part
of the verse, it is hard to avoid the conclusion that the
cleansing power of fire is partly in mind. If this be so,
then the Baptism with the Holy Spirit which is

*primarily* an energizing process, is also a revealing, refining, consuming, illuminating process, and one by which we are made to glow with love to God, and love to man, and love to souls.

5. We will get a still clearer and fuller view of what the Baptism with the Holy Spirit is, if we will notice what this Baptism does. This is stated concisely in Acts 1:8. "Ye shall receive *power* after that the Holy Ghost is come upon you; and ye shall be witnesses," etc. The Baptism with the Holy Spirit imparts "*power*" power for service. This power will not manifest itself in precisely the same way in each individual. This is brought out very clearly in 1 Cor. 12:4-13, K. V.: "Now there are diversities of gifts but the same spirit. For to one is given, through the Spirit, the word of wisdom; and to another the word of knowledge, according to the same spirit; to another faith, in the same spirit; and to another gifts of healing, in the one spirit; to another diverse kinds of tongues; but all these worketh the one and the same spirit, dividing to each one severally even as He will." In my early study of the Baptism with the Holy Spirit, I noticed that in many instances those who were so baptized "spoke with tongues," and the question came often into my mind: if one is baptized with the Holy Spirit will he not speak with tongues? But I saw no one so speaking, and I often wondered, is there any one today who actually is baptized with the Holy Spirit. This twelfth chapter of 1st Corinthians cleared me up on that, especially when I

found Paul asking of those who had been baptized with the Holy Spirit: "Do all speak with tongues?" (1 Cor. 12:30.) But I fell into another error, namely, that any one who received the Baptism with the Holy Spirit would receive power as an evangelist, or as a preacher of the Word. This is equally contrary to the teaching of the chapter, that "there are *diversities of gifts*, but the one Spirit." There are three evils arising from the mistake just mentioned. First, disappointment. Many will seek the Baptism with the Holy Spirit, expecting power as an evangelist, but God has not called them to that work, and the power that comes from the Baptism with the Holy Spirit manifests itself in another way in them. Many cases of bitter disappointment and almost despair have arisen from this cause. The second evil is graver than the first: presumption. A man whom God has not called to the work of an evangelist, or minister, rushes into it because he has received, or thinks he has received, the Baptism with the Holy Spirit. Many a man has said: "All a man needs to succeed as a preacher is the Baptism with the Holy Spirit." This is not true. He needs a call to that specific work, and he needs the study of the Word of God that will prepare him for the work. The third evil is still greater: indifference. There are many who know they are not called to the work of preaching. For example, a mother with a large family of children knows this. If then, they think that the Baptism with the Holy Spirit simply imparts power to preach, it is a matter of no personal concern to them; but when we come to see the truth that, while the Baptism with the Spirit imparts power, the way in which that power will be manifested, depends upon the work to which God has called us, and that no efficient work can be done without it, then the mother will see that she equally with the preacher needs this Baptism—needs it for that most important and hallowed of all work, to bring up her children "in the nurture and admonition of the Lord." I have recently met a very happy mother. A few months ago she heard of the Baptism with the Holy Spirit, sought it and received it. "Oh," she joyfully exclaimed as she told me the story, "Since I received it, I have been able to get into the hearts of my children which I was never able to do before."

It is the Holy Spirit Himself who decides how the power will manifest itself in any given case: "the spirit dividing to each one severally even as He will." (1 Cor. 12:11 R. V.) We have a right "to desire earnestly the greater gifts" (1 Cor. 12; 31.), but the Holy Spirit is sovereign, and He not we, must determine in the final issue. It is not for us then to select some gift, and then look to the Holy Spirit to impart the self-chosen gift; it is not for us to select some field of service and then look to the Holy Spirit to impart to us power in that field which we, and not He, have chosen. It is rather for us to recognize the Divinity and sovereignty of the Spirit, and put ourselves unreservedly at His disposal; for Him to select the gift that "He will" and impart to us that gift; for Him to select for us the field that "He will" and impart to us the power that will qualify us for the field He has chosen. I once knew a child of God, who, hearing of the Baptism with the Holy Spirit and the power that resulted from it, gave up at a great sacrifice, the secular work in which he was engaged, and entered upon the work of an evangelist. But the expected power in that line did not follow. The man fell into great doubt and darkness, until he was led to see that the Holy Spirit divideth "to each one severally, even as He will." Then giving up selecting his own field and gifts, he put himself at the Holy Spirit's disposal for Him to choose. In the final outcome the Holy Spirit did impart to this man power as an evangelist and a preacher of the Word. We must then surrender ourselves absolutely to the Holy Spirit to work as He will.

But, while the power that the Baptism with the Holy Spirit brings, manifests itself in different ways in different individuals, there will always be power. Just as surely as a man is baptized with the Holy Spirit there will be new power, a power not his own, "the power of the Highest!" Religious biography abounds in instances of men, who have worked along as best they could, until one day they were led to see there was such an experience as the Baptism with the Holy Spirit, and to seek it and obtain it. From that hour there came into their service a new power that utterly transformed its character. Finney, Brainerd and Moody are a few of the many cases in point.

Cases of this character are not confined to a few exceptional men, they are becoming common. The writer has personally met and corresponded with hundreds during the past twelve months, who could testify definitely to the new power that God had granted them through the Baptism with the Holy Spirit. These hundreds of men and women were in all branches of Christian service. Many of them were ministers of the gospel, others mission workers, others Y, M. C. A. secretaries, others Sunday school teachers, others personal workers, others fathers and mothers. Nothing could exceed the clearness, confidence and joy fullness of many of these testimonies. What we have in promise in the words of Christ many have, and all may have, in glad experience: "Ye shall receive power, after that the Holy Ghost is come upon you."

6. There is another but closely related result of the Baptism with the Holy Spirit in Acts 4:31. "They were all filled with the Holy Ghost, and they spake the Word of God *with boldness*." The Baptism with the Holy Spirit imparts to those who receive it new liberty and fearlessness in testimony for Christ. The same Peter, who before his baptism with the Holy Spirit, cowered at the maid's charge that he was one of Jesus' disciples (John 18:17) after his baptism with the Holy Spirit, faces the very council that put Jesus to death and says: "The God of our fathers raised up Jesus whom ye slew and hanged upon a tree." (Acts 5:30) The natural timidity and constraint of many a

man today, vanishes when he is filled with the Holy
Spirit, and with great boldness and liberty and
fearlessness he gives his testimony for Christ.

7. The Baptism with the Holy Spirit causes the
one who receives it to be occupied with God and
Christ and spiritual things. On the day of Pentecost it
was "the mighty works of God," (Acts 2:11) of which
the Spirit-filled men and women spoke. Peter's
sermon on that day is all about Christ, and especially
about His resurrection. (Acts 2:22-36, compare also
Acts 4:8-10, 31, 33). When Saul of Tarsus had been
filled with the Holy Spirit, "straightway in the
synagogues he *proclaimed Jesus.*" (Acts 9:17, 20).
When Cornelius and his household were baptized
with the Holy Spirit they began at once to "magnify
God" (Acts 10: 44-46). Men who are baptized with
the Holy Ghost do not talk much about self, but very
much of God, and especially about Christ. This is
naturally so, as it is the Spirit's office to "bear
witness of" and "glorify" Christ. ( John 15:26, R. V.
16:14.) Paul says that the result of being "filled with
the Holy Spirit" is that men speak "to one another in
psalms and hymns and spiritual songs, singing and
making melody with their hearts to the Lord." (Eph.
5: 18, 19.) Worldly songs loose their charm to one
who is baptized with the Holy Spirit; he is occupied
with Christ.

To sum up the contents of this chapter: The
Baptism with the Holy Spirit is the Spirit of God

The Baptism with The Holy Spirit
coming upon the believer, taking possession of his
faculties, imparting to him gifts not naturally his
own, but which qualify him for the service to which
God has called him.

## CHAPTER II

# THE NECESSITY AND POSSIBILITY OF THE BAPTISM WITH THE HOLY SPIRIT

Shortly before Christ was received up into heaven, having committed the preaching of the gospel to His disciples, He laid upon them this very solemn charge concerning the beginning of the great work He had committed to their hands: "Behold, I send forth the promise of my Father upon you; but tarry ye in the city, until ye be clothed with power from on high." (Luke 24:49, R. V.) There is no doubt as to what Jesus meant by the "promise of my Father" for which they were to wait before beginning the ministry which He had intrusted to them; for in Acts1:4, 5, we read that Jesus "charged them not to depart from Jerusalem, but to wait for *the promise of the Father*" which, said he, "Ye heard from me: for John indeed baptized with water: but ye shall be *baptized with the* Holy Ghost not many days hence." "The promise of the Father," through which the enduement of power was to come, was the Baptism with the Holy Spirit. (Comp. Acts 1:8). Christ then strictly charged His disciples not to presume to

The Baptism with The Holy Spirit

undertake the work to which He had called them until they had received as the necessary and all essential preparation for that work, the Baptism with the Holy Spirit. The men to whom Jesus said this, seemed to have already received very thorough preparation for the work in hand. They had been to school to Christ Himself for more than three years. They had heard from His own lips the great truths that they were to proclaim to the world. They had been eye-witnesses of His miracles, of His death and of His resurrection and were about to be eye-witnesses of His ascension. The work before them was simply to go forth to proclaim what their own eyes had seen and what their own ears had heard from the lips of Christ Himself. Were they not fully prepared for this work? It would seem so to us. But Christ said: "No. You are so utterly unprepared you must not stir a step yet. There is a further preparation, so all-essential to effective service, that you must abide at Jerusalem until you receive it. This further preparation is the Baptism with the Holy Spirit. When you receive that—and *not until then*—you will be prepared to begin the work to which I have called you." If Christ did not permit these men, who had received so rare and unparalleled a schooling for the work to which He had so definitely and clearly called them, to undertake this without receiving in addition to that the Baptism with the Holy Spirit, what is it for us to undertake the work to which He has called us until we have received, in addition to any amount of schooling we may have had for the work, the Baptism with the Holy Spirit? Is it not most daring presumption?

But this is not all. In Acts 10:38, we read "how God anointed Jesus of Nazareth with the Holy Ghost and with power: who went about doing good, and healing all that were oppressed of the devil." When we look into the gospels for an explanation of these words, we find it in Luke 3:21, 22; 4:1, 14, 15, 18, 21. We find that at the Baptism of Jesus at Jordan *as* He *prayed*, the Holy Spirit came upon Him. Then, "*full* of the Holy Ghost," He has the temptation experience. Then , "*in the power of Spirit*" He begins His ministry, and proclaims himself "*anointed* to preach" because "*the Spirit of the Lord is upon* Him." In other words, Jesus the Christ, never entered upon the ministry for which He came into this world until He was baptized with the Holy Spirit. If Jesus Christ, who had been supernaturally conceived through the Holy Spirit's power, who was the only begotten Son of God, who was divine, very God of very God, and yet truly man; if such an one, "leaving us an example that we should follow in His steps," did not venture upon the ministry for which the Father had sent Him until thus baptized with the Holy Ghost, what is it for us to dare to do it? If, in the light of these recorded facts, we dare to do it, it seems like an offence going beyond presumption. Doubtless it has been done in ignorance by many, but can we plead ignorance any longer? *The Baptism with the Holy Spirit is an absolutely necessary preparation for effective service*

## The Baptism with The Holy Spirit

*for Christ along every line of service.* We may have a
very clear call to service, as clear it may be as the
Apostles had, but the charge is laid upon us, as upon
them, that before we begin that service we must
"tarry until ye be clothed with power from on high."
This enduement with power is through the Baptism
with the Holy Spirit. There are certainly few greater
mistakes that we are making today, than that of
setting men to teach Sunday-school classes, and do
personal work, and even to preach the gospel, simply
because they have been converted and received a
certain amount of education—perhaps including a
college and seminary course—but have not as yet
been baptized with the Holy Spirit. Any man who is
in Christian work, who has not received the Baptism
with the Holy Spirit, ought to stop his work right
where he is, and not go on with it until he has been
"clothed with power from on high." But what will
our work do while we are waiting? What did the
world do those ten days while the early disciples
were waiting? They alone knew the saving truth, yet,
in obedience to the Lord's command, they were
silent. The world was no loser. When the power came
they accomplished more in one day than they would
have accomplished in years, if they had gone on in
presumptuous disobedience to Christ's charge; so
will we after we have received the Baptism with the
Holy Spirit accomplish more in one day than we ever
would in years without His power. Days spent in
waiting, if it were necessary, would be well spent, but
we shall see further on that there is no need that we

spend days in waiting. It may be said that the
Apostles had gone out on missionary tours during
Christ's lifetime before they were baptized with the
Holy Spirit. This is true, but that was before the Holy
Ghost was given, and before the charge, "tarry until
ye be clothed with power from on high" was given.
After that it would have been disobedience and
presumption to have gone forth without this
enduement, and we are living today after the Holy
Ghost has been given and after the charge to "tarry
until clothed" has been given.

We come now to the question of the Possibility
of the Baptism with the Holy Spirit. Is the Baptism
with the Holy Spirit for us? This is a question that has
a most plain and explicit answer in the Word of God.
In Acts 2:39, R. V., we read: "For to you is the
promise, and to your children and to all that are afar
off, even as many as the Lord our God shall call unto
Him." What is "the promise" of this passage?
Turning back to the fourth and fifth verses of the
preceding chapter we read: "Wait for *the promise* of
the Father, which, saith He, ye have heard of Me. For
John truly baptized with water; but *ye shall be
baptized with the Holy Ghost* not many days hence."
Again in the thirty-third verse of the second chapter
we read: "Having received of the Father *the promise*
of the Holy Ghost." It would seem to be perfectly
clear that "the promise" of the thirty-ninth verse must
be the same as "the promise" of the thirty-third verse
and "the promise" of the fourth and fifth verses of the

The Baptism with The Holy Spirit

preceding chapter; *i. e.*, the promise of the Baptism with the Holy Spirit. This conclusion is rendered absolutely certain by the context: "Repent and be baptized every one of you in the name of Jesus Christ unto the remission of your sins, and *ye shall receive the gift of the Holy Ghost*. For to you is the promise," etc. The promise then of this verse is the promise of the gift or Baptism with the Holy Ghost. (Comp. Acts 10:45 with Acts 11:15, 16, to prove that "the gift of the Holy Ghost" is the same as "the Baptism with the Holy Ghost.") Who is this gift for? "To you," says Peter to the Jews whom he was immediately addressing. Then looking over their heads to the next generation, "And to your children." Then looking down all the coming ages of the Church's history to Gentile as well as Jew: "And to all that are afar off, even as many as the Lord our God shall call unto Him." The Baptism with the Holy Spirit is for every child of God in every age of the Church's history. If it is not ours in experimental possession, it is because we have not taken (the exact force of the word translated "receive" in verse 38 is *take*) what God has provided for us in our exalted Savior. (Acts 2:33;John 7:38, 39.) A minister of the gospel once came to me after a lecture on the Baptism with the Holy Spirit, and said: "The church to which I belong, teaches that the Baptism with the Holy Spirit was for the Apostolic age alone." "It matters not," was replied, "what the church to which you belong, or the church to which I belong, teaches. What says the Word of God?" Acts 2:39 was read: "To you is the promise, and to your children, and to all that are afar off, even as many as the Lord our God shall call unto Him." "Has He called you?" I asked. "Yes He certainly has." "Is the promise for you?" "Yes, it is." And it was. And it is for every child of God who reads these pages. What a thrilling thought it is that the Baptism with the Holy Spirit, the enduement with *power* from *on high* is for us, is FOR ME individually! But that unspeakably joyous thought has its solemn side. If I may be baptized with the Holy Spirit I *must* be. If I am baptized with the Holy Spirit, then will souls be saved *through my instrumentality* who are not so saved if I am not so baptized. If then I am not willing to pay the price of this Baptism, and therefore am not so baptized, I am responsible before God for all the souls that might have been saved, but were not saved, through me, because I was not baptized with the Holy Spirit. I oftentimes tremble for my brethren in Christian work and myself. Not because we are teaching deadly error to men; some are guilty of even that, but I do not refer to that now. Not that we are not teaching the full truth as it is in Jesus. It must be confessed that there are many, who do not teach positive error, who do not preach a full gospel, but I do not refer to that. I tremble for those who are preaching the truth, the truth as it is in Jesus, the gospel in its simplicity, in its purity, in its fullness, but preaching it "in persuasive words of wisdom" and not "in demonstration of the Spirit and of power" (1 Cor. 2:4, R. V.), preaching it in the energy of the flesh and not in the power of the Holy Spirit. There is nothing more deadly than the gospel without the Spirit's power. "The letter killeth, but the Spirit giveth life." It is awfully solemn business preaching the gospel either from the pulpit or in more quiet ways. It means death or life to those who hear, and whether it means death or life depends very largely on whether we preach it without or with the Baptism with the Holy Spirit. We must be baptized with the Holy Spirit.

Note 1. It is sometimes argued that "the Baptism with the Holy Spirit" was for the purpose of imparting miracle working power, and for the Apostolic age alone. In favor of this position it is asserted that the Baptism with the Holy Spirit was followed quite uniformly by miracles. The untenableness of this position is seen: (1) By the fact, that Christ Himself asserted that the purpose of the Baptism with the Holy Spirit was to impart power for witnessing—not especially power to work miracles. (Acts 1:5, 8; Luke 20:48, 49.) (2) By the fact, that Paul distinctly taught that there were diversities of gift, and that "workings of miracles" was only one of the manifold manifestations of the Baptism with the Holy Spirit. (Cor. 12:4, 8-10.) (3) By the fact, that Peter distinctly asserts that "the gift of the Holy Ghost," "the promise," is for all believers in all generations (Acts 2:88, 89), and it is evident from a comparison of Acts 2:39 with Luke 24:49; Acts 1:4, 5; 2: 33, and of Acts 2:38 with Acts 10:45 and Acts 11:15, 16, that each of these two expressions, "the promise," and "the gift of the Holy Ghost," refers to the Baptism with the Holy Spirit. If we take miracles in the broad sense of all results wrought by supernatural power, then it is true that each one baptized with the Holy Spirit does receive miracle-working power; for each one so baptized does receive a power not naturally his own: supernatural power, God's own power. The result of the Baptism with the Holy Spirit that was most noticeable and essential was convincing, convicting and converting power. (Acts 2:4, 37, 41. Acts 4:8-13. Acts 4:81, 38. Acts 9:17, 20-22.) There seem to have been no displays of miracle-working power immediately following Paul's Baptism with the Holy Spirit, even though he became so singularly gifted in this direction at a later day—it was power to witness for Jesus as the Son of God that he received in immediate connection with the Baptism with the Holy Spirit (Acts 9:17, 20-22.)

Note 2. It is taught by some, that the Baptism with the Spirit is for the church as a whole and not for the individual believer, and that the whole church was baptized at Pentecost, and that therefore it is unwarrantable for individual believers today to pray or seek for a baptism with the Spirit. But the scriptures very dearly disprove this position. The record of Pentecost is that "it sat upon *each one* of them. (Acts 2:3, R. V.) Not on the Church collectively, but upon each believer individually. This position is further shown to be untenable by the fact that the Apostles inquired of individual churches and believers whether they had received the Holy Spirit, (Acts 8:15, 16; 19:2,) and found, in some instances at least, that they had not, whatever the church as a whole may have received.

Note 3. An eminent Bible teacher has these strange comments to make on Acts 8: "If the Samaritan can believe and rejoice in that belief for some time without the gift of the Holy Spirit in his outward manifestations, if He cannot be so given except by the imposition of an apostle's hands, is it not plain that the time has begun when He will no longer be present in His extraordinary displays? The twelve could not go the world over to lay hands on millions." We answer, no it is not plain at all. Indeed it contradicts the plain teaching of Scripture. Acts 19:1-6, came long after (perhaps 17 years) Acts 8:12-16. Furthermore, though the Samaritans did "believe and rejoice in that belief for some time without the gift of the Holy Spirit," it was so important that they have it that this was the first and principal thing the apostles attended to upon their arrival. Further still the question itself contains a statement that is contrary to fact, viz: "He cannot be so given except by the imposition of an apostle's hands." In the case of Saul of Tarsus it was "a certain disciple" who imposed his hands (Acts 9:10, 17). In the case of the household of Cornelius there was no imposition of hands at all (Acts 10:44). It may be said "these instances are exceptional." With some people everything that does not fit a preconceived theory is exceptional. Further still this position contradicts flatly Peter's statement in Acts 2:89. The above writer continues: "There is no hint that the Romans had this particular gift. The same is true of other churches." Let anyone who fancies this to be so read Rom. 12:6-8; 1 Cor. 12: 7-18, 28-81; Gal. 3:2. (Here Paul refers to a definite, conscious experience of the receiving of the Holy Spirit as a proof of God's pleasure with "the hearing of faith"); Eph. 1:13, 14; 4:7, 11. So far from its being evident that "the gift was not intended to be universal or permanent," it is evident that it was intended to be universal and permanent, and that men do not enter into it simply because of their unbelief. It is amazing the number of theories that have been proposed to relieve the consciences of those who are troubled at the wide gulf between their experience and the plain teaching of the Acts of the Apostles. A better way to relieve the conscience would be to find out the conditions and make one's own this blessed experience.

There is abundant present day experience confirming the teaching of the Word along these lines. While many have been trying to work out some "subtle" exegetical method of "explaining away" the seeming meaning of the Bible; others have simply believed it, and know by the indisputable proof of experience that a child of God may today "be baptized with the Holy Spirit," and that he does "receive power after that the Holy Ghost is come upon" him. God grant that the present reader of this

The Baptism with The Holy Spirit
book may claim this glorious "birthright" of the
children of God for himself. The refining verities of
believing experience immeasurably transcend the
refined subtleties of unbelieving exegesis.

# CHAPTER III

# HOW THE BAPTISM WITH THE HOLY SPIRIT IS OBTAINED

We have now come to a place where there is a deep sense that we must be baptized with the Holy Spirit. The practical question confronts us: how can we obtain this baptism with the Holy Spirit which we so sorely need? This question also the Word of God answers very plainly and very explicitly. There is pointed out in the Bible a path, consisting of seven simple steps, which any one who will can take, and whoever takes these seven steps will, with absolute certainty, enter into this blessing. This statement may seem very positive, but the Word of God is equally positive regarding the outcome of taking these steps which it points out. All seven steps are stated or implied in Acts 2:38: "Repent ye, and be baptized every one of you in the name of Jesus Christ unto the remission of your sins, *and ye shall receive* the gift of the Holy Ghost." The first three steps are brought out with especial definiteness and distinctness in this verse. The others, which are clearly implied in the verse, are brought out more explicitly by other passages to which we shall refer later.

# The Baptism with The Holy Spirit

1. The first two steps are found in the word " repent." What does "repent" mean? *Change your mind*; change your mind about what? About God, about Christ, about sin. As to what the change of mind is about in any given case must be determined by the context. Here the first and most prominent thought is a change of mind about Christ. Peter has just brought against his hearers the awful charge that they had crucified Him whom God had made both Lord and Christ. "Pricked in their heart" by this charge, carried home by the power of the Holy Spirit, his hearers had cried out, "Men and brethren, what shall we do?" "Repent," Peter answered. Change your mind about Christ. Change from a Christ-hating and Christ crucifying attitude of mind to a Christ accepting attitude of mind. Accept Jesus as Savior, Christ and Lord. *This then is the first step toward the Baptism with the Holy Spirit: Accept Jesus as Savior, Christ and Lord.* Have you taken this step? Have you accepted Jesus as your Savior? Are you relying wholly upon His atoning work for pardon? Relying solely upon the fact that He bore your sins, for acceptance before God? ( 1 Pet. 2:24; 2 Cor. 5:21.) There are many professed Christians who are not doing this, many who are trying to add some works of their own to the finished work of Christ, as a ground of acceptance with God, But Paul says that we receive the Spirit not "by the works of the law," but by "the hearing of faith." (Gal. 3:2.) If you have accepted Jesus as your Savior, have you also

accepted Him as your Christ and Lord? That is, have you surrendered the absolute control of your life to Him? We will hear more of this further on in the fourth step.

2. The second step is also found in the word "repent." While the change of mind about Jesus is the first and prominent thought, there must also be a change of mind about sin. A change of mind from a sin loving or sin-indulging attitude of mind to a sin-hating and sin-renouncing attitude of mind. This is the second step: renounce sin, all sin, every sin. Here we come upon one of the commonest obstacles to receiving the Holy Spirit—Sin. Something is held on to that in our inmost hearts we more or less definitely fee to be not pleasing to God. If we are to receive the Holy Spirit, there must be very honest and very thorough heart searching. We cannot do satisfactory heart searching ourselves, God must do it. If we wish to receive the Holy Spirit, we should go alone with God and ask Him to search us thoroughly and bring to light anything that displeases Him. (Ps. 139:23, 24.) Then we should wait for Him to do it. When the displeasing thing is revealed, it should be put away at once. If, after *patient* and *honest* waiting, nothing is brought to light, we may conclude there is nothing of this kind in the way, and proceed to the further steps. But we should not conclude this too hurriedly. It is not time lost to wait long before God as He sends the searching light of His Spirit and Word into the innermost recesses of our heart and life. It is a painful

but salutary process. The sin that hinders the blessing may be something that appears very small and insignificant in itself. Mr. Finney tells of a young woman who was in deep concern regarding the Baptism with the Holy Spirit. Night after night she agonized in prayer, but the desired blessing did not come. One night as she was in prayer there came up before her some matter of head adornment that had often troubled her before; putting her hand to her head, she took the pins out and threw them away, and immediately the blessing came. This was a small matter in itself, a matter that would not have appeared to many as sin, but yet a matter of controversy between this woman and God, and when this was settled the blessing came. It may be something that you regard as very, very insignificant that is shutting you out of the Baptism with the Holy Spirit. Surely it is not insignificant if it is doing that. Whatever the controversy you have with God, have done with it. "Whatsoever is not of faith is sin" (Rom. 14:23), and it matters not how little the thing may be, if there are questions regarding it, it must be put away, if we are to have the Baptism with the Holy Spirit. How many have agonized and prayed for the Baptism with the Holy Spirit without any result, until the obstructing sin was removed and then the blessing came. *The second step then toward the Baptism with the Holy Spirit is to put away every sin.*

3. The third step is found in this same verse: "*Be baptized in the name of Jesus Christ unto the*

*remission of your sins.*" It was immediately after His baptism that the Holy Spirit descended upon Jesus. (Luke 3:21, 22.) In His baptism, Jesus though Himself sinless, humbled Himself to take the sinner's place, and then God highly exalted Him by the giving of the Holy Spirit and by the audible testimony; "Thou art my beloved son; in thee I am well pleased." So we must humble ourselves to make open confession of our sin and renunciation of it and acceptance of Jesus Christ, in God's appointed way, by baptism. The Baptism with the Holy Spirit is not for the one who secretly takes his place as a sinner and believer in Christ, but for the one who does so openly. Of course, the Baptism with the Holy Spirit may precede water baptism; as in the case, of the household of Cornelius. (Acts 10:47.) But this was evidently an exceptional case, and water baptism immediately followed. I have little doubt that there have been those, among Christians who did not believe in or practice water baptism — as, for example, "the Friends" or "Quakers"—who have had and given evidence of the Baptism with the Holy Spirit, but the passage before us certainly presents the normal order.

4. The fourth step is clearly implied in the verse we have been studying, (Acts 2:38) but it is brought out more explicitly in Acts 5:32: "The Holy Ghost, whom God hath given to them *that obey Him*," *The fourth step is obedience.* What does obedience mean? It does not mean merely doing some of the things, or

many of the things, or most of the things, that God bids us do. It means *total surrender to the will of God*. Obedience is an attitude of the will lying back of specific acts of obedience. It means that I come to God and say: "Heavenly Father, here I am and all I have. Thou hast bought me with a price and I acknowledge Thine absolute ownership. Take me and all I have, and do with me whatsoever Thou wilt. Send me where Thou wilt, use me as Thou wilt. I surrender myself and all I possess absolutely, unconditionally, forever, to Thy control and use." It was when the burnt offering, *whole*, no part held back, was laid upon the alter that "there came forth fire from before the Lord" and accepted the gift (Lev. 9:24); and it is when we bring ourselves a *whole* burnt offering to the Lord, and lay ourselves thus upon the altar, that the fire comes and God thus accepts the gift. Here we touch upon the hindrance to the Baptism with the Holy Spirit in many lives: there is not total surrender, the will is not laid down, the heart does not cry: "Lord, where Thou wilt, what Thou wilt, as Thou wilt." One man desires the Baptism with the Holy Spirit that he may preach or work with power in Boston, when God wishes him in Bombay. Another, that he may preach to popular audiences, when God wishes him to plod among the poor. A young woman at a convention expressed a strong desire that some one would speak on the Baptism with the Holy Spirit. The address went home with power to her heart. She had been for some time in deep travail of soul when I asked her what it was that she desired. "Oh," she cried, "I cannot go back to Baltimore until I am baptized with the Holy Spirit." "Is your will laid down?" "I don't know." "You wish to go back to Baltimore to be a Christian worker?" "Yes." "Are you willing to go back to Baltimore and be a servant girl if that is where God wishes you?" "No I am not." "Well, you will never get the Baptism with the Holy Spirit until you are. Will you lay your will down?" "I can't." "Are you willing God should lay it down for you?" "Yes." "Well, then, ask Him to do it." The head was bowed in brief but earnest prayer. "Did God hear that prayer?" "He must have, it was according to His will; He did." "Now ask Him for the Baptism with the Holy Spirit." Again the head was bowed and the brief, earnest prayer ascended to God. There was a brief silence, and the agony was over, the blessing had come—when the will was surrendered. There are many who hold back from this total surrender because they fear God's will. They are afraid God's will may be something dreadful. Remember who God is. He is our Father. Never an earthly father had so loving and tender a will regarding his children as He has toward us. "No good thing will He withhold from them that walk uprightly." ( Ps. 84:11 ) . "He that spared not His own Son, but delivered Him up for us all, how shall He not with Him also freely give us all things?" There is nothing to be feared in God's will. God's will will always prove in the final outcome the best and sweetest thing in all God's universe.

The Baptism with The Holy Spirit
## The Baptism with The Holy Spirit

5. The fifth step is found in John 7:37-39: "Jesus stood, and cried, saying, if any man *thirst*, let him come unto me, and drink. He that believeth on me, as the Scripture hath said, out of his belly shall flow rivers of living water. But this spake He of the Spirit, which they that believe on him should receive." There is also a very suggestive passage in Isaiah, the forty-fourth chapter and third verse; "I will pour water upon him that is *thirsty*. . .I will pour my Spirit upon thy seed." Matt. 5:6 is also closely related to these two passages: "Blessed are they which do hunger and *thirst* after righteousness, for they shall be filled." What does it mean to thirst? When one thirsts there is but one cry: "Water! water! water!" Every pore in the body seems to have a voice and cry out "water." So when our hearts have one cry: "the Holy Spirit, the Holy Spirit, the Holy Spirit," then it is that God pours floods upon the dry ground, pours His Spirit upon us. *This then is the fifth step—intense desire for the Baptism with the Holy Spirit.* To what a pitch of longing the early disciples had been brought by the tenth day of their eager waiting! and their thirsty souls were filled that day when "Pentecost was fully come." As long as one thinks he can get along somehow without the Baptism with the Holy Spirit, as long as he casts about for something in the way of education, or cunningly concocted methods of work, to take its place, he is not going to receive it. There are many ministers who are missing the fullness of power God has for them, simply because they are not willing to admit the lack there has been

all these years in their ministry. It is indeed a humiliating thing to confess, but that humiliating confession would be the precursor of a marvelous blessing. But there are not a few, who, in their unwillingness to make this wholesome confession, are casting about for some ingenious device of exegesis to get around the plain and simple meaning of God's Word, and thus they are cheating themselves of that fullness of the Spirit's power which God is so eager to bestow upon them; and furthermore, they are imperiling the eternal interests of the souls that are dependent upon their ministrations, that might be won for Christ, if they had the power of the Holy Spirit which they might have. But there are others whom God in His grace brought to see that there was a something their ministry lacked, and this something nothing less than that all-essential Baptism with the Holy Spirit, without which one is utterly unqualified for acceptable and effective service. They have humbly and frankly confessed their lack. Sometimes they have been led to the God-taught resolution that they would not go on in their work until this lack was supplied. They have waited in eager longing upon God the Father for the fulfillment of His promise, and the result has been a transformed ministry for which many have risen to bless God.

It is not enough that the desire for the Baptism with the Holy Spirit be intense; it must also be pure. There is a desire for the Baptism with the Holy Spirit that is entirely selfish. Many a one has an intense desire for the Baptism with the Holy Spirit, simply that he may be a great preacher, or great personal worker, or renowned in some way as a Christian. It is simply his own gain or glory that he is seeking. After all it is not the Holy Spirit that he seeks, but his own honor, and the Baptism with the Holy Spirit simply as a means to that end. One of the subtlest and most dangerous snares into which Satan leads us, is that where we are seeking the Holy Spirit, this most solemn of all gifts, for our own ends. The desire for the Holy Spirit must not be in order to make that sublime and divine Person the servant of our low ends, but for the glory of God. It must arise from a recognition that God and Christ are being dishonored by my powerless ministry and by the sin of the people about me, against which I now have no power, and that He will be honored, if I have the Baptism with the Spirit of God. One of the most solemn passages in the New Testament bears upon this point. (Acts 8:18-24, R. V.) "When Simon saw that through the laying on of the Apostles' hands the Holy Ghost was given, he offered them money, saying: Give me also this power, that on whomsoever I lay my hands, he may receive the Holy Ghost." Here was a strong desire on Simon's part, but it was entirely unhallowed and selfish, and Peter's terrific answer is worthy of note and meditation. Is there not many a one today who, with equally unhallowed and selfish purpose desires the Baptism with the Holy Spirit? Each one who is desiring and seeking the Baptism with the Holy Spirit, would do well to ask himself *why* he desires it. If you find that it is merely for your own gratification or glory, then ask God to forgive you the thought of your heart, and to enable you to see how you need it for His glory, and to desire it to that end.

6. The sixth step is shown in Luke 11; 13; "If ye then, being evil, know how to give good gifts unto your children, how much more shall your heavenly Father give the Holy Spirit to them that *ask* Him." *The sixth step is to ask.* Definite asking for a definite blessing. When Christ has been accepted as Savior and Master, and confessed as such; when sin has been put away; when there has been the definite, total surrender of the will; when there is real and holy desire; then comes the simple act of asking God for this definite blessing. It is given in answer to earnest, definite, specific, believing prayer. It has been earnestly contended by some that we should not pray for the Holy Spirit. They reason this out in this way: "The Holy Spirit was given to the Church at Pentecost as an abiding gift." This is true, and what was given to the Church each believer must appropriate for himself. It has been well said on this point, that God has already given Christ to the world (John 3:16), but that each individual must appropriate Him by a personal act to get the personal advantage of the gift, and so must each individual personally appropriate God's gift of the Holy Spirit to get the personal advantage of it. But it is argued still further

The Baptism with The Holy Spirit

that each believer has the Holy Spirit. This is also true in a sense. "If any man have not the Spirit of Christ, he is none of His. (Rom. 8:9.) But as we have already seen, it is quite possible to have something, yes much, of the Spirit's presence and work in the heart, and yet come short of that special fullness and work known in the Bible as the Baptism or Filling with the Holy Spirit. In answer to all specious reasonings on this subject we put the simple statement of Christ: "How much more shall your heavenly Father give the Holy Spirit to them that *ask* Him." At a convention at which the author was announced to speak on this subject, a brother said to him: "I see you are to speak on the Baptism with the Holy Spirit." "Yes." "It is the most important subject on the programme; now be sure and tell them not to pray for the Holy Spirit." "I shall certainly not tell them that; for Jesus said: 'How much more shall your heavenly Father give the Holy Spirit to them that *ask* Him.'" "Oh, but that was before Pentecost." "How about Acts 4:31? Was that before Pentecost or after?" "After it, of course." "Well, read it." It was read: "When they had *prayed*, the place was shaken where they were assembled together, and they were all filled with the Holy Ghost." "How about the eighth chapter of Acts? Was that before Pentecost or after?" "After, of course?" "Well, read the fourteenth to the seventeenth verses." The verses were read: "Peter and John, when they were come down, *prayed* for them, that they *might receive the Holy Ghost*; for *as yet He was fallen upon none of them*, . . . and they

~ 46 ~

received the Holy Ghost." Against all inferences is this clear teaching of the Word by precept and example, that the Holy Spirit is given in answer to prayer. It was so at Pentecost; it has been so since. Those whom I have met who give most evidence of the Spirit's presence and power in their life and work believe in praying for the Holy Spirit. It has been the author's unspeakable privilege to pray with many ministers and Christian workers for this great blessing, and afterward to learn from them or from others of the new power that has come into their service, none other than the power of the Holy Spirit.

7. The seventh and last step is found in Mark 11:24. "What things soever ye desire, when ye pray, *believe* that ye receive them, and ye shall have them." God's most positive and unqualified promises must be appropriated by faith. In Jas. 1:5, we read: "If any of you lack wisdom, let him ask of God that giveth to all men liberally and upbraideth not; and it shall be given him." Now, that is certainly positive and unqualified enough, but listen to what the writer says next: "But let him ask *in faith, nothing wavering*, for he that wavereth is like a wave of the sea driven with the wind and tossed. For let not that man think that he shall receive anything of the Lord." There must then be faith in order to make our own the most positive and unqualified promises of God, such as that in Luke 11:13, and Acts 2:38, 39. Here then we discover the cause of failure, in many cases, to enter into the blessing of the Baptism with the Holy Spirit.

The Baptism with The Holy Spirit

The failure is because the last step is not taken—the simple step of faith. They do not believe, they do not confidently expect, and we have another instance of how men "Entered not in because of unbelief." (Heb. 4: 6.) There are many, very many, who are kept out of this land of milk and honey just by this unbelief. It should be added that there is a faith that goes beyond expectation, a faith that just puts out its hand and takes what it asks. This is brought out very clearly by the R. V. of Mark 11:24. "All things whatsoever ye pray and ask for, believe that ye have received them and ye shall have them." I remember how greatly I was perplexed by this rendering of the R. V. when I first noticed it. On examining the Greek of the passage I saw that the R. V. was correct, but what did it mean? It seemed like a singular confusion of the tenses. "Believe that *ye have* (already) *received* them, and ye *shall have* them." This seeming enigma was solved long after, while studying the First Epistle of John. I read in the fifth chapter, fourteenth and fifteenth verses: "This is the boldness which we have toward Him, that, if we ask anything according to His will, He heareth us: and if we know that He heareth us whatsoever we ask, we know that *we have* the petitions which we have asked of Him." (R. V.) When I ask anything of God the first thing to find out is: is this petition according to His will? When that is settled, when I find it is according to His will, when, for example, the thing asked is definitely promised in His Word—then I know the prayer is heard, and I know further, "I have the petition which I have asked

of Him." "I know it because He plainly says so, and
what I have thus appropriated on simple, childlike
faith in His naked Word "I shall have" in actual
experience. When one who has a clear title to a piece
of property deeds it to me, it is mine as soon as the
deed is properly executed and recorded, though it
may be some time before I enter into the
experimental enjoyment of it. I have it in the one
sense as soon as the deed is recorded. I shall have it
in the other sense later. In like manner, as soon as we,
having met the conditions of prevailing prayer, put up
to God a petition for "anything according to His
will," it is our privilege to know that the prayer is
heard, and that the thing which we have asked of Him
is ours. Now apply this to the Baptism with the Holy
Spirit. I have met the conditions of obtaining this
blessing already mentioned. I simply, definitely, ask
God, the Father, for the Baptism with the Holy Spirit.
Then I stop and say: was that prayer "according to
His will?" Yes, Luke 11:13 says so. "If ye then being
evil, know how to give good gifts unto your children,
how much more shall your heavenly Father give the
Holy Spirit to them that ask Him?" Acts 2:38, 39
says: "Repent ye, and be baptized every one of you in
the name of Jesus Christ unto the remission of your
sins; and ye shall receive the gift of the Holy Ghost.
For to you is the promise, and to your children, and to
all that are afar off, even as many as the Lord our
God shall call unto Him." (R. V.) It is clear that the
prayer for the Baptism with the Holy Spirit is
"according to His will," for it is definitely and plainly

promised. I know then that the prayer is heard, and that *I have the petition which I have asked of him*, (1 John 5:14, 15, R. V.) That is, I have the Baptism with the Holy Spirit. I have then the right to arise from my knees and say, on the all-sufficient authority of God's Word: "I have the Baptism with the Holy Spirit," and *afterwards* I shall have in experimental enjoyment what I have appropriated by simple faith; for God has said, and He cannot lie, "All things whatsoever ye pray and ask for, believe that ye have received them, *and ye shall have them.*"

Any reader of this book may at this point lay it down, and, if Christ has been accepted as Savior and Lord, and openly confessed as such in God's way, and if sin has been searched out and put away, and if there has been total surrender of the will and of self to God, and if there is a true desire, for God's glory, to be baptized with the Holy Spirit—if these conditions have been met, you may get down just now before God, and ask him to baptize you with the Holy Spirit, and you can then say, when the prayer has gone up: "That prayer was heard, I have what I have asked, I *have the baptism with the Holy Spirit*," and you have a right to get up and go out to your work, assured that in that work you will have the Holy Spirit's power. But some one will ask: "Must I not know that I have the Baptism with the Holy Spirit before I begin the work?" Certainly, but how shall we know? I know of no better way of knowing anything than by God's Word. I would believe God's Word before my feelings any day. How do we deal with an inquirer who has accepted Christ, but who lacks assurance that he has eternal life? We do not ask him to look at his feelings, but we take him to some such passage as John 3:36. We tell him to read it and he reads: "He that believeth on the Son hath everlasting life." "Who says that?" we ask. "God says it." "Is it true?" "Oh, certainly it is true; God says it." "Who does God say has everlasting life?" "He that believeth on the Son." "Do you believe on the Son?" "Yes," "What have you then?" "O, I don't know, I don't feel yet that I have eternal life." "But what does God say?" "He that believeth on the Son hath everlasting life." "Are you going to believe God or your feelings?" We hold the inquirer right there until on the simple, naked Word of God, feeling or no feeling, he says: "I know I have eternal life because God says so," and afterwards the feeling comes. Deal with yourself in this matter of the Baptism with the Holy Spirit just as you deal with an inquirer in the matter of assurance. *Be sure you have met the conditions,* and then simply *ask, claim, act.* But some one will say: "Will it be just as it was before; will there not be some manifestation?" Most assuredly there will be some manifestation. "To each one is given the manifestation of the Spirit to profit withal." (1 Cor. 12:7, R. V.) But what will the character of the manifestation be and where shall we see it? It is at this point that many make a mistake. They have, perhaps, read the life of Mr. Finney or of Jonathan Edwards, and recall how great waves of electric emotion swept over these men until they were obliged to ask God to withdraw His hand lest they die from the ecstasy. Or they have gone to some meeting, and heard testimonies to similar experiences, and they expect something like this. Now I do not deny the reality of such experiences. I cannot. The testimony of such men as Finney and Edwards is to be believed. There is a stronger reason why I cannot deny them. But while admitting the reality of these experiences, I would ask, where is there a single line of the New Testament that describes any such experience in connection with the Baptism with the Holy Spirit? Every manifestation of the Baptism with the Holy Spirit in the New Testament was in new power in service. Look, for example, at 1 Cor. 12, where this subject is treated in the most thorough way, look also at Acts 2:4; 4:31; 4:33; 9:17, 22 and note the character of the manifestations mentioned. It is quite probable that the Apostles had similar experiences to those of Finney and Edwards and others, but, if they had, the Holy Spirit kept them from recording them. It is well He did; for, if they had told of such things, we would have looked for these things rather than the more important manifestation of power in service.

But another question will be asked: "Did not the Apostles wait ten days, and may we not have to wait?" The Apostles were kept waiting ten days, but the reason is given in Acts 2:1: "When the Day of Pentecost was now come" (literally was being fulfilled, R. V. Marg.) In the eternal purposes and plans of God, and in the Old Testament types, the Day of Pentecost was set as the time for the giving of the Holy Spirit, and the Spirit could not be given until the Day of Pentecost was fully come, but we read of no waiting after Pentecost. In Acts 4: 31 there was no waiting. "*When they had prayed* the place was shaken where they were assembled together, and they were all filled with the Holy Ghost," In Acts 8 there was no waiting. When Peter and John came down to Samaria, and found that none of the young converts had been baptized with the Holy Spirit, they "prayed for them, that they might receive the Holy Ghost," and they did then and there. (Acts 8:15, 17). Paul of Tarsus was not obliged to wait, in the ninth chapter of the Acts. Ananias came in and told him of this wondrous gift, and baptized him, and laid his hands upon him, and "*straightway* in the synagogue he proclaimed Jesus, that He is the Son of God." (Acts 9:17, 20). There was no waiting in Acts 10. Before Peter had fairly gotten through his sermon the Baptism with the Holy Spirit came. (Acts 10:44-46; Comp. Chap. 11:15,16.) In the nineteenth chapter of the Acts there was no waiting. As soon as Paul had declared to the Ephesian disciples the gift of the Holy Spirit, and the conditions were met, the blessing followed. (Acts 19:1-6.) Men have to wait only when they do not meet the conditions, when Christ is not fully accepted, or sin is not put away, or there is not total surrender, or true desire, or definite prayer, or simple faith, just taking upon the naked Word. The absence of some of these things keeps many waiting for more than ten days sometimes. But there is no need that any reader of this book wait ten hours. You can have the Baptism with the Holy Spirit just now, if you will. A young man once came to me in great earnestness about this matter. "I heard of the Baptism with the Holy Spirit," he said, "some time ago, and have been seeking it, but have not received it." "Is your will laid down?" "I am afraid that is the trouble." "Will you lay it down?" "I am afraid I cannot." "Are you willing God should lay it down for you?" "Yes." "Ask Him to." We knelt in prayer, and he asked God to lay down his will for him. "Did God hear that prayer?" "He must have, it was according to His will." "Is your will laid down?" "It must be." "Then ask God for the Baptism with the Holy Spirit." He did this. "Was that prayer according to His will?" "Yes." "Was it heard?" "It must have been." "Have you the Baptism with the Holy Spirit?" "I don't feel it." "That is not what I asked you; read those verses again." The Bible lay open before him at 1 John 5:14, 15, and he read: "This is the confidence we have in Him that, if we ask anything according to His will. He heareth us." "Wait a moment; was that prayer according to His will?" "It certainly was." "Was it heard?" "It was." "Read on." "And if we know that He hears us whatsoever we ask, we know that we have the petitions that we desired of Him." "Know what?" "That we have the petitions we desired of Him." "What was the petition?" "The Baptism with the Holy Spirit." Have you it?" "I don't feel it, but

R. A. Torrey

God says so, and I must have." A few days later I met
him again, and asked if he really had received what
he took on simple faith. With a happy look in his face
he answered, "Yes." I lost sight of him for perhaps
two years, and then found him preparing for the
ministry and already preaching, and God was
honoring his preaching with souls saved, and a little
later used him with others as a means of great
blessing to the theological seminary where he was
studying. He had also decided to serve Christ in the
foreign field. What he claimed on simple faith and
received, any reader of this book can claim and
receive in the same way.

# The Baptism with The Holy Spirit

# CHAPTER IV

# "FRESH BAPTISMS WITH THE HOLY SPIRIT" OR THE REFILIING WITH THE HOLY SPIRIT.

In the second chapter of the Acts of the Apostles, fourth verse, we read: "They were all filled with the Holy Ghost, and began to speak," etc. This was the fulfillment of Acts 1:5. "Ye shall be baptised with the Holy Ghost not many days hence." One of those mentioned by name as being "filled with the Holy Ghost," (Acts 2:4), or "baptised with the Holy Ghost" (Acts 1:5), at this time was Peter. Turning over to the fourth chapter, the eighth verse, we read: "Then Peter, filled with the Holy Ghost, said unto them," etc. Here Peter experienced a new filling with the Holy Spirit. Again, in the thirty-first verse of this same chapter, we read: "When they had prayed the place was shaken where they were assembled together; and they were all filled with the Holy Ghost." Peter is named as one of this company (verses 19 and 23), so we see that Peter here experienced a third filling with the Holy Spirit. It is evident that it is not sufficient that one be once "baptized with the Holy Spirit." As new emergencies of service arise, there must be new fillings with the

Spirit. The failure to realize this has led to most sad and serious results in many a man's service. He has been baptized at some period in his life with the Holy Spirit, and strives to get though his whole future life in the power of this past experience. It is largely for this reason, that we see so many men who once unquestionably worked in the Holy Spirit's power, who give little evidence of the possession of that power today. For each new service that is to be conducted, for each new soul that is to be dealt with, for each new service for Christ that is to be performed, for each new day and each new emergency of Christian life and service, we should definitely seek a new filling with the Holy Spirit. I do not deny that there is an "anointing that abideth," (1 John 2:27), nor the permanency of the gifts that the Holy Spirit bestows; I simply assert with clear and abundant Scripture proof, to say nothing of proof from experience and observation, that this gift must not be "neglected," (1 Tim. 4:14) but rather "kindled anew" or "stirred into flame" (2 Tim. 1:6, R. V. Marg.); and that repeated fillings with the Holy Spirit are necessary to continuance and increase of power. Now arises the question, ought these new *fillings* with the Holy Spirit to be called "fresh *Baptisms* with the Holy Spirit?" While, on the one hand, it must be admitted that in Acts 2:4, the expression, "filled with the Holy Ghost." is used to describe the experience promised in Acts 1:5, in the words: "Ye shall be baptized with the Holy Ghost," and that therefore the two expressions are to this extent synonymous; on the other hand, it should be noticed, that the expression, "Baptized with the Holy Spirit," is nowhere used in the Bible of any experience but the first, and that, furthermore, the word "baptized" of itself suggests an initial or initiatory experience. While, therefore, we stand for the truth that those who speak of "fresh baptisms with the Holy Spirit" are aiming at, it would seem wisest to follow the uniform Bible usage, and speak of the experiences that succeed the first, as being *"filled* with the Holy Spirit," and not as being *"baptized* with the Holy Spirit"

# The Baptism with The Holy Spirit

# CHAPTER V

## HOW SPIRITUAL POWER IS LOST

Any discussion of the Baptism with the Holy Spirit, and the power which results from it, would be incomplete, if attention were not called to the fact that spiritual power may be lost.

One of the strangest and saddest stories of the Old Testament history, is that of Samson. It is also one of the most instructive. He was by far the most remarkable man of his day. The grandest opportunities were open to him, but after striking temporary victories, his life ended in tragic failure, all through his own inexcusable folly. Time and again it is said of him that "the Spirit of the Lord came mightily upon him," and in the power of that Spirit he wrought to the astonishment of his people and the discomfiture of the enemies of the Lord; but in Judges 16:19, 20, we see him deserted of the Lord, though unconscious of it, his strength gone from him, and he about to be taken into wretched captivity, the sport of the godless, and to die with the enemies of the Lord a violent and dishonored death.

Unfortunately Samson is not the only man in Christian history, who, having once known the power of the Holy Spirit, has afterward been shorn of this power and laid aside. There have been many Samsons, and I presume there will be many more — men whom God has once used mightily and has afterward been forced to lay aside. One of the saddest sights on earth is such a man. Let us consider when it is that the Lord departs from a man or withdraws His power from him, or in other words, "How power is lost."

1. *First of all God withdraws His power from men when they go back upon their separation to Him.* This was the precise case with Samson himself. (Judges 16:19, Comp. Num. 6:2, 5.) His uncut hair was the outward sign of his Nazarite vow by which "he separated himself unto the Lord." The shearing of his hair was the surrender of his separation. His separation given up he was shorn of his power. It is at this same point that many a man today is shorn of his power. There was a day when he separated himself unto God. He turned his back utterly upon the world and its ambitions, its spirit, its purposes; he set himself apart to God as holy unto Him, to be His, for God to take him and use him and do with him what He would. God has honored his separation, He has anointed him with the Holy Ghost and power. He has been used of God. But Delilah has come to him. The world has captured his heart again. He has listened to

the world's siren voice, and allowed her to shear him of the sign of separation. He is no longer a man separated, or wholly consecrated, to the Lord, and the Lord leaves him. Are there not such persons among those who read this? Men and women the Lord once used, but He does not use you now. You may still be outwardly in Christian work, but there is not the old time liberty and power in it, and this is the reason—you have been untrue to your separation, to your consecration to God; you are listening to Delilah, to the voice of the harlot, to the world and its allurements. Would you get the old power back again? There is but one thing to do. Let your hair grow again as Samson did. Renew your consecration to God.

2. *Power is lost through the incoming of sin.* It was so with Saul, the son of Kish. The Spirit of God came upon Saul and he wrought a great victory for God. (1 Samuel 11:6, ff.) He brought the people of God forward to a place of triumph over their enemies, who had held them under for years. But Saul disobeyed God in two distinct instances (1 Samuel 18: 13, 14; 15:3, 9-11, 23), and the Lord withdrew His favor and His power, and Saul's life ended in utter defeat and ruin. This is the history of many men whom God has once used. Sin has crept in. They have done that which God has told them not to do, or they have refused to do that which God bade them do, and the power of God has been withdrawn. The one who has known God's power in service, and

would continue to know it, must walk very softly before Him. He must be listening constantly to hear what God bids him do or not do. He must respond promptly to the slightest whisper of God. It would seem as if any one who had once known God's power would rather die than lose it. But it is lost through the incoming of sin. Are there those among the readers of this book who are passing through this dreadful experience of the loss of God's power? Ask yourself if this be the reason; has sin crept in somewhere? Are you doing something, some little thing, perhaps, that God tells you not to do? Are you leaving undone something God bids you do? Set this matter right with God and the old power will come back. David was guilty of an awful sin, but when that sin was confessed and put away, he came to know again the power of the Spirit. (Ps. 32:1-5; 51:11-13.)

If we would continuously know the power of God we should go often alone with Him, at the close of each day at least, and ask Him to show us if any sin, anything displeasing in His sight, has crept in that day, and if He shows us that there has, we should confess it and put it away then and there.

3. *Power is lost again through self-indulgence.* The one who would have God's power must lead a life of self-denial. There are many things which are not sinful in the ordinary understanding of the word sin, but which hinder spirituality and rob men of power. I do not believe that any man can lead a

luxurious life, over-indulge his natural appetites, indulge extensively in dainties, and enjoy the fullness of God's power. The gratification of the flesh and the fullness of the Spirit, do not go hand in hand. "The flesh lusteth against the Spirit, and the Spirit against the flesh: and these two are contrary the one to the other." (Gal 5:17.) Paul wrote, "I keep under my body, and bring it into subjection." (1 Cor. 9:27, see R. V, Greek. Note also Eph. 5:18.)

We live in a day when the temptation to the indulgence of the flesh is very great. Luxuries are common. Piety and prosperity not seldom go hand in hand, and, in many a case, the prosperity that piety and power have brought has been the ruin of the man to whom it has come. Not a few ministers of power have become popular and in demand. With the increasing popularity has come an increase of pay and of the comforts of life. Luxurious living has come in, and the power of the Spirit has gone out. It would not be difficult to cite specific instances of this sad truth. If we would know the continuance of the Spirit's power, we need to be on guard to lead lives of simplicity, free from indulgence and surfeiting, ever ready to "endure hardness, as a good soldier of Jesus Christ." (2 Tim. 2:3.) I frankly confess I am afraid of luxury;—not as afraid of it as I am of sin but it comes next as an object of dread. It is very subtle but a very potent enemy of power. There are devils today that "go not out but by prayer and fasting."

The Baptism with The Holy Spirit

4. *Power is lost through greed for money*. It was through this that a member of the original Apostolic company, the twelve whom Jesus Himself chose to be with Him, fell. The love of money, the love of accumulation, got into the heart of Judas Iscariot, and proved his ruin. "The love of money is a root of all kinds of evil," (1 Tim. 6:10, R. V.) but one of the greatest evils of which it is the root is that of the loss of spiritual power. How many a man there is today who once knew what spiritual power was, but money began to come. He soon felt its strange fascination. The love for accumulation, covetousness, the love for more, little by little took possession of him. He has accumulated his money honestly; but it has absorbed him, and the Spirit of God is shut out and His power has departed. Men who would have power, need to have the words of Christ. "Take heed and beware of covetousness," writ large and graved deep upon their hearts. One does not need to be rich to be covetous. A very poor man may be very much absorbed in the desire for wealth—just as much so as any greedy millionaire.

5. *Power is lost through pride*. This is the subtlest and most dangerous of all the enemies of power. I am not sure but that more men lose their power at this point, than at any of those mentioned thus far. There is many a man who has not consciously gone back upon his consecration, he has not let sin, in the sense of conscious doing of that which God forbade or conscious refusal to do that which God commanded,

creep into his life, he has not given way to self-indulgence; he has utterly, persistently and consistently refused the allurements of money accumulation, but still he has failed; *pride has come in*. He has become puffed up because of the very fact that God has given him power and used him; puffed up, it may be, over the consistency and simplicity and devotion of his life; and God has been forced to set him aside. God cannot use a proud man. (1 Pet. 5:5.) "God resisteth the proud and giveth grace to the humble." The man who is puffed up with pride, self-esteem, cannot be filled up with the Holy Spirit. Paul saw this danger for himself. God saw it for him, and "lest he be exalted above measure, through the abundance of the revelations, there was given to (him) a thorn in the flesh, the messenger of Satan to buffet (him), lest (he) should be exalted above measure." (2 Cor. 12:7.) How many men have failed here! They have sought God's power, sought it in God's way, it has come. Men have testified of the blessing received through their word, and pride has entered and been indulged, and all is lost. Moses was the meekest of men, and yet he failed at this very point. "Must we fetch you water out of this rock?" he cried, and then and there God laid him aside. (Num. 20: 10-12.) If God is using us at all, let us get down very low before Him. The more he uses us the lower let us get. May God keep His own Words ringing in our ears: "Be clothed with humility, for God resisteth the proud, and giveth grace to the humble." (1 Pet. 5:5.)

6. *Power is lost through neglect of prayer.* It is in prayer especially that we are charged with the energy of God. It is the man who is much in prayer into whom God's power flows mightily. John Livingston spent a night with some Christians in conference and prayer. The next day June 21st, 1630, he so preached at the Kirk of Shotts, that the Spirit fell upon his hearers in such a way that five hundred could either date their conversion or some remarkable confirmation from that day forward. This is but one instance among thousands to show how power is given in prayer. Virtue or power is constantly going from us, as from Christ (Mark 5:30), in service and blessing; and if power would be maintained, it must be constantly renewed in prayer. When electricity is given off from a charged body it must be recharged. So must we be recharged with the Divine energy, and this is effected by coming into contact with God in prayer. Many a man whom God has used has become lax in his habits of prayer, and the Lord departs from him and his power is gone. Are there not some of us who have not today the power we once had, and simply because we do not spend the time on our faces before God that we once did?

7. *Power is lost through neglect of the Word.* God's power comes through prayer, it comes also through the Word (Ps. 1:2, 3; Josh. 1:8.) Many have known the power that comes through the regular, thoughtful, prayerful, protracted meditation upon the

Word, but business and perhaps Christian duties have multiplied, other studies have come in, the Word has been in a measure crowded out, and power has gone. We must meditate daily, prayerfully, profoundly upon the Word if we are to maintain power. Many a man has run dry through its neglect.

I think the seven points mentioned give the principal ways in which spiritual power is lost. I think of no others. If there is one dread that comes to me more frequently than any other, it is that of losing the power of God. Oh, the agony of having known God's power, of having been used of Him, and then of having that power withdrawn, to be laid aside as far as any real usefulness is concerned. Men may still praise yon, but God can't use you. To see a perishing world around you and to know there is no power in your words to save. Would not to die be better than that? I have little fear of losing eternal life. Every believer in Christ has that already. I am in the hand of Jesus Christ, and in the hand of God the Father, and no one can pluck me out of Their hand, (John 10:28, 29), *but* I see so many men from whom God has departed, men once eminently used of God, I walk with fear and trembling, and cry unto Him daily to keep me from the things that would make the withdrawal of His power necessary. But what those things are I think He has made plain to me, and I have tried in the words here written to make them plain to both you and myself. To sum them up they are these: the surrender of our separation, sin, self-indulgence, greed for money, pride, the neglect of prayer, and the neglect of the Word. Shall we not, by God's grace, from this time be on our guard against these things, and thus make sure of the continuance of God's power in our life and service until that glad day comes when we can say with Paul: "I have fought a good fight, I have finished my course, I have kept the faith; henceforth there is laid up for me a crown of righteousness, which the Lord, the righteous judge, shall give me at that day," (2 Tim. 4:7, 8), or better yet with Jesus, "I have glorified Thee on the earth, having accomplished the work which Thou hast given me to do." (John 17:4, R. V.)

## FINIS.

R. A. Torrey

## Check Out the Other Great Works
of
## R. A. Torrey

The Importance And Value Of Proper Bible Study
How Properly to Study and Interpret the Bible

Anedotes and Illustations

Difficulties In The Bible
Alleged Errors and Contradictions

The Baptism with The Holy Spirit

How to Pray

What The War Teaches
or The Greatest Lessons of 1917

How To Bring Men To Christ

Revival Addresses

How to Succeed in the Christian Life

How to Study the Bible for Greatest Profit

Printed in Great Britain
by Amazon